PERFORMANCE
EDITIONS

DEBUSSY
CHILDREN'S CORNER

Edited and Recorded by Christopher Harding

T0082065

To access companion recorded performances online, visit:
www.halleonard.com/mylibrary

Enter Code
7413-0311-5940-7418

On the cover:
Child in White
by Pierre Auguste Renoir
(1841–1919)

ISBN 978-1-4234-5289-8

G. SCHIRMER, *Inc.*

DISTRIBUTED BY
HAL•LEONARD®
CORPORATION
7777 W. BLUEMOUND RD. P.O. BOX 13819 MILWAUKEE, WI 53213

www.musicsalesclassical.com
www.halleonard.com

CONTENTS

ABOUT CHILDREN'S CORNER

CLAUDE DEBUSSY (1862–1918)

I think that every teacher who loves music must be delighted by exploring anew with their students the world of Debussy's *Children's Corner*. The work's inspiration was nothing less than the surpassing tenderness Debussy cherished for his daughter Claude-Emma (his only child, born in 1905 when Debussy was forty-three years old). Because of this, *Children's Corner* can serve as an invitation to a deeper musical relationship between student and teacher, one in which both can enrich their understanding of and love for sound—what sound means, and what we mean when we produce certain sounds.

In this music we have every reason to encourage the imagination of our students in specific detail. After all, Debussy was writing about a real person whom he adored; that love shines forth from every note, every rest, every dash in the score. After such a labor of love and great thought, do we owe Debussy anything less than our complete and thoughtful imagination as we strive to understand and then communicate through our performances his love for "Chou-Chou," as he so fondly called her? Not to do so is to decline the opportunity to learn a profound lesson about life from one of our greatest musicians. I would go so far as to say that in searching out the truth found in *Children's Corner* we can learn what it is to become alive in our art. We naturally hope to achieve this in all the repertoire we explore, but a satisfying and compelling performance of this work demands it.

I hope it is apparent from these words that although some of the movements of *Children's Corner* are among the easiest of Debussy's works to learn and to play, these pieces were not written for children or inexperienced pianists. They are meant, rather, for sensitive souls who can grasp the tenderness of a loving father for his daughter, and who have the ability to paint those feelings in sound. These requirements need not specify an age or skill level before attempting any part of the suite. But it might be well to keep in mind that they do indicate what should be the result of our study.

As a jumping off point, we might consider Debussy's words to his friend Louis Laloy on Claude-Emma's birth: "This joy has quite bowled me over and still bewilders me!"[1] Debussy's joy deepened into a relationship of such tenderness that he missed his daughter exceedingly whenever he was obliged to travel. In 1910, he sent this series of post cards to her from Vienna:

"First Card

To Chou-Chou,   Vienna, 2nd December 1910

The memoirs of a far-away Croche.
["Croche" is a nickname which Debussy took for himself.]

Once upon a time there was a daddy who was living in exile...

(To be continued in the next.)

Second Card

...and he longed every day for his little Chou-Chou.

Third Card

> The folk of this town watched his passing by and murmured: 'Why does this gentleman look so sad in our gay and lovely town?'

Fourth Card

> Then Chou-Chou's daddy went into a shop kept by a very ugly man and his still uglier daughter. Daddy took off his hat politely, made signs like a deaf-mute to ask for the prettiest postcards on which to write to his dear little girl. The old man was quite overcome; as for his daughter, she died instantly.

Fifth Card

> The same papa went back to his hotel, wrote a story which made the goldfish weep and put all his deep love into the signature below which is his most glorious title.

> LEPAPADECHOUCHOU

(As quoted by P. Vallery-Radot in *Lettres et telegrammes de Claude Debussy à sa femme Emma*, pub. Flammarion.)"[2]

This charming correspondence came after the *Children's Corner* had been written, a process which took place over the years 1906–1908. It began with a commission from a Paris piano teacher for a piece to be included in a new piano method, which Debussy titled "Sérénade à la poupée." He then decided to expand this idea into a whole suite of portraits of Chou-Chou and the world of her toys. Every parent of a two or three year old toddler knows the joys of that age—and the desire to increase that joy through presents. These pieces are presents for and about Chou-Chou, but they are not meant to match or illustrate faithfully her "childish" abilities. I imagine that parents who love their children with great tenderness, but whose understanding of them is colored by their own artistic refinement, in general seek to direct their children's growth along the same artistic paths. Here we see Debussy encouraging, by example, those qualities Chou-Chou must have shared with him: extraordinary sensitivity to sound, imagination, and attention to detail. She must also have shared his sophisticated humor and understated wit. The English titles of *Children's Corner* are a reference to Chou-Chou's English governess. The naively charming drawings by Debussy himself which adorn the cover of the earliest editions must have been drawn for Chou-Chou's amusement. What else could induce Debussy to illustrate his own work with such images?

Debussy knew his daughter for only twelve years; he died in 1918 after a very painful struggle with cancer and its fledgling treatments. But life was more uncertain for everyone in those days. Chou-Chou herself died very suddenly little more than a year after her father, leaving behind only the *Children's Corner* as a testimony to the love he bore for her.

—*Christopher Harding*

PERFORMANCE NOTES

TOWARD AN UNDERSTANDING OF PLAYING DEBUSSY

Style

In studying Debussy's music, our attention to detail and the interpretation of his markings must be as meticulous as when we approach the music of Haydn and Mozart. Debussy had a real abhorrence of pianists who performed his music with cavalier freedom. On several occasions he expressed his desire for a faithful interpreter, one who would not yield to the temptation of doing what is not written in the indulgence of "personal interpretation." It is true that we can't and should not avoid real differences of performance among us, but we must strive to create in our minds an exact understanding of what is written.

An example of this might be the "railroad tracks" or "double dashes" we find at the end of certain passages marked with tempo fluctuations (i.e., *un peu retenu* in m. 21 of "Doctor Gradus ad Parnassum"). These dashes indicate that the *un peu retenu* is finished and do not imply a break in the sound or a lift of the hand from the keyboard, as might be assumed in other styles of music. (Other specific details, especially of articulation, are treated below.)

This emphasis on the exact and precise nature of his music is very important to a correct understanding of Debussy's place within what we call "Impressionism" in music. Debussy actually disliked this term when applied to his works, and perhaps with good cause. When we think of Impressionism in visual art and music, we tend to think of a wash of sound and color. We might even be tempted to turn to a copious amount of pedaling (referring to any of the three pedals) to help us achieve this "washiness." Impressionistic piano music is certainly very colorful and often uses much pedal, but those colors and use of pedals can and must be very precise—even when we want to be carried away with great washes of sound, as often happens in Ravel. Impressionism embraces a wide palette and combination of colors, but these are never blurred indiscriminately. We seek to create a "precise impression," through the precision of our interpretation.

This sense of the "precise impression" is very typical of the French aesthetic. It often manifests itself in a certain reserve or distance from its subject, eschewing emotional display, and seeks an elegant refinement of execution and effect. German music is typically highly expressive, but French music is not—unless the composer asks for it, as in the *Children's Corner*. At such moments we must consider whether the *expressif* quality is best expressed through a change of sound, the taking of time, or both. But, it must be thought about and planned, especially by those of us who are not born and bred in the French aesthetic. We Americans tend to be impatient with the French world of elegant reserve, of subdued and refined emotion. Instead, we prefer to hold back very little in the name of "being real," pursuing straightforward and open honesty. Our culture is suspicious of reserve. But the beauty of entering into the music of another culture is the chance to grow in the understanding of our own, and to emerge as a greater human being. I don't believe that Debussy would call his music "reserved" in any way, but we might perceive it that way at first. The challenge is to understand and delight in its beauty on its own terms, to learn the lessons Debussy has to teach us, and not to appropriate the notes for our own purposes.

I have said that these pieces are written about a child, but I don't believe that they are to be performed as if played by a child. I believe that the sheer beauty and tenderness of the performance must be considered more important than a literal fidelity to any supposed storyline. We could liken this idea to the images of children that a painter such as Renoir has left us. No doubt the children in his paintings had runny noses, headaches, and problems with table manners on occasion, but he doesn't show us all that. Instead, he captures the beauty of the child (and the idea of a child's beauty) through light and color, and so captures our hearts through the experience of a precise visual and (here is the great mystery) emotional impression of beauty. I feel that Debussy does the same.

Sound and Color

Although the movements of the *Children's Corner* are among some of the easiest pieces written by Debussy to play and learn, they should not be underestimated in terms of the technique required to play them, because of the demands for precise sound production. Sound originates in the imagination and the demands of our ear (by which I mean that we must have a precise idea of what kind of sound we want), but colors are produced from the fingertips by means of touch, through the use of the damper and una corda pedals, and through precise voicing. One of the most notable characteristics of Debussy's music is his use of many different layers of voicing and sound, very clearly sculpted and colored through a variety of touches, often within the same hand. But even this ought not to be exaggerated. An excellent example would be the opening measures of "Doctor Gradus ad Parnassum" and the layers of sound possible in the arpeggiated chords of the right hand. (This passage is explained in greater detail in the notes to the individual movements.)

In seeking out a colorful voicing or balance among certain layers of sound, it is useful to play the various voices of a chord or passage with two hands before trying it with one hand. I feel it is important to get the sound in my ear first, by whatever means, before trying for its "proper" execution. If the ear demands it, the fingers and hands will find a way to produce it.

I also practice a lot without pedal to hear the honest truth about what kind of sound, color, and voicing the fingers are, or are not, producing. Then the pedals can be added as enhancements. Of course, we use a lot of pedal for all sorts of purposes—harmonic, melodic, coloristic, etc. But pedaling should be finely coordinated with the work of the fingers as part of the overall sound, not as the producer of sound or color.

The range of dynamics in any given piece should be strictly observed and understood in their context. Dynamics are relative to one another and to the room in which we are playing, but they are also emotional and indicative of feeling and expression. For example, a *mezzo forte* that occurs in a piece which rarely rises above a *piano* is a dynamic of great importance. But in the execution of dynamics we must not allow ourselves to be too exuberant or direct. Rather, everything is more moderate, with fine gradations of sound and color—not straight, but not straightforward, not matter of fact. An excellent example is the opening of "Jimbo's Lullaby" wherein the sound by itself creates the mood because of its low register. We don't have to "add" expression or exaggerated shapes of the line.

Articulation

Debussy's approach to the keys was to be one with them—to be attached to them as extensions of our sensitive hands and fingers. This approach, combined with his famous admonition that the piano ought to be played as if it had no hammers, might lead us to conclude that he desired a "mushy" or weakly articulated sound, but this is untrue. Even a cursory glance at any of his scores reveals a plethora of staccato notes and accents of various kinds. And then, there are portato notes ♪ ♪ ♪ which are to be played as long staccatos with a legato shaping of the phrase. In the case of an individual portato note ♪, the tenuto asks us to hold the staccato a little longer, functioning the same way as the slur over a group of staccatos. It should be noted that staccato sixteenths are shorter than staccato eighths, which are in turn shorter than staccato quarters, and so on. Accents which lay on their side > are to be "leaned into," emphasized with a little more weight. Accents that look like a sharp vertical wedge ^ are played in the sharp manner we commonly associate with accents; and, of course, there are all sorts of combinations of these symbols.

When interpreting these articulation symbols in context, the main considerations are length and attack. What kind of attack seems to be called for here: sharp or gentle, fast or slow, direct or caressing? Secondly, how long should the note sound? Should the eighth notes which begin "The snow is dancing" have the length of a sixteenth note? We should also keep in mind that the length of a note may not directly affect the speed of the attack, but might have a direct relationship to the attack. This is for the pianist to decide. Pianists are especially guilty of neglecting the "ends" of their notes. We tend to be concerned first and foremost with the attack or "beginning" of a note, placing it exactly in time with the pulse. For those of us who are more experienced, we might be highly concerned with the sound of a note as it is singing. But, the precise release of a note is just as important for crispness and clarity of expression.

As an example of the problem of grappling with Debussy's specific articulations, we may examine mm. 3–4 from "Golliwogg's cake walk":

Golliwogg's cake walk, mm. 3–4

We notice in m. 3 that the C-flat is articulated with a wedge accent, or played sharply. How is this different from the staccato wedges that articulate the final chord of m. 4? Debussy must want a much shorter note than the quarter note of the previous measure, irrespective of the dynamic. The dynamic is loud, of course, but not because of the accent. The *sforzando* takes care of that bit of information. And, of course, we must be careful to make sure that the C-flat on beat two of m. 4 is "leaned into" with a different (and gentler) articulation than the C-flat of the previous measure, thus creating a bigger surprise for us when the final chord "stamps" for our attention.

Pedaling

Debussy leaves us next to no explicit instruction in his scores of how he wanted us to use the pedals. There are some exceptions. The "Serenade for the Doll" provides two of them in this suite, but we are forced to resort to some sleuthing in order to figure out Debussy's intentions. Often times Debussy will indicate his use of pedal by writing whole notes which can't be held with the fingers (such as m. 9 of "Jimbo's Lullaby"), or by the use of slur markings which tie over to nothing in particular (but this is rare in the *Children's Corner*). Sometimes pedaling can be used as a kind of glue for help in chord leaps (i.e., "Jimbo's Lullaby," mm. 41–42).

Debussy considered pedaling to be similar to breathing. I feel that the important thing about pedaling is not "when to push it down," but rather "when to release or change it, and how," much like swimmers have to be concerned with how they take breaths as they swim. Pedaling, whether using the damper pedal or the una corda, is perhaps the most individual of all things pianistic, very difficult to notate and reproduce from pianist to pianist or from piano to piano. Pedaling is often used to color harmonies and melodies, and sometimes for rhythmic accentuation; but, there are in addition to these uses many different levels of pedaling for both the damper and the una corda pedals. Sensitive pianists will find themselves using quarter, half, three-quarters, full pedals, barely touching the pedal, etc. All these uses and countless more are at our disposal, limited only by our imagination and penchant for exploration.

There are two crucial points about pedaling that should be made here. The first is very basic, but I see it in many advanced students and so feel that I should make a statement about it. Pedaling is best accomplished with the ball of the foot (that fleshy area just behind the toes) resting on the end of the pedal, with the heel on the floor. A great deal of sensitivity and "oneness with the pedal" is sacrificed when students pedal with the toes or with the instep of their foot.

Secondly, great attention should be paid to the "point of engagement" of the damper pedal. We should learn to listen for the point at which the dampers begin to damp the strings as we release the damper pedal. When we become sensitive to this moment in sound, we can begin to make use of the incredible subtleties to be had by very quick and shallow half and quarter pedal changes, hovering around this "point of engagement." I have found the following exercise to be useful. It is very much like learning to drive a manual transmission car, but mercifully without the danger of stalling out:

> Play any note and depress the damper pedal to hold the note while you release the key. (One could do this in reverse order, but I like hearing the change in sound from the single set of strings vibrating to the entire set of piano strings vibrating in sympathy with the struck note.) Next, slowly release the pedal until you hear that the dampers have damped the strings completely, all the while noting the change of sound as the dampers come closer to the strings. At the point where the note stops ringing, cease to release the pedal. This is the "point of engagement," as I call it, the point where the dampers are completely touching the strings. Now, release the pedal entirely. Often we are surprised at the remaining distance and how far we have to depress the pedal before the effect kicks in. The frustrating thing is that this distance is different on every piano.

Similar exercises can be developed for exploring the una corda—for instance, repeating a certain note with different depths of pedal. With sensitivity and knowledge of how these pedals can change the sound with subtle accuracy, we can make use of various depths of pedal for different sounds: full deep pedal for harmonic richness, shallow pedal for coloristic affects, etc. This is all dependent on the individual's ear and a great deal of individual experimentation by teacher and student.

Pedaling does have a connection to dynamics. The damper pedal, in particular, produces a certain volume of sound that has to be dealt with if one is after an intimate effect. In this case, we might consider using less pedal. Sometimes we can pedal through rests because they are "articulation rests" which tell us to take our hand off the keyboard or to release a certain note for articulation purposes, not rests intended to produce silence. But other times we need to be careful to let rests speak clearly. Sometimes we must exaggerate our articulation in order to speak through the pedal. This is often the case when using una corda, but we must also make sure to speak clearly with our fingers while using the damper pedal. Our fingers ought not to get weak simply because our foot is coming on strong. For instance, when I use the una corda in combination with a decrescendo, it is not as a substitute for shaping the decrescendo with my fingers. It just helps to change the quality of the sound (i.e., mm. 18–19 of "Jimbo's Lullaby").

The use of pedals in Debussy is both extremely important and extremely individual. This is certainly a reason why Debussy has left us so little explicit guidance, and his judgment in this matter is probably best. We have therefore respected his practice on this point, leaving pedaling decisions up to the active imagination of the performer. However, in an appendix I have included an example of my pedalings for "Doctor Gradus ad Parnassum," with the caveat that they were found to be most useful on a specific piano on a specific day in a specific hall. Rather than a reference of authority, please consider them examples of what can be done with the pedals to contribute to a successful performance, and use them as a springboard for your own imagination.

Inner Voices and Fingering

Another important point to mention in connection with several movements of the *Children's Corner* is Debussy's use of bass lines or inner voices as structural unifiers. This is typical of much of his piano music and can be very useful for grading tempo and color changes, and establishing harmonic goals and direction. We see examples of such structural unifiers in the bass voice of mm. 32–45 of "Doctor Gradus ad Parnassum" and the inner voices of mm. 81–92 of "Golliwogg's cake walk." Both examples are discussed in the notes to individual movements, but others can be found and used by those attuned to their possible presence.

The fingerings contained herein are suggestions only. Fingerings vary according to size and flexibility of different hands, and Debussy himself believed that fingerings were intensely personal. In the preface to his Études, Debussy proclaims that in this matter one is never better served than by one's own self. But just as pedaling is useful for certain colors, so I find that certain fingerings encourage certain colors from my hand, and I use it to create a true legato. There are far fewer possibilities for fingerings than for pedalings, so I have offered some suggestions for those who might need some workable ideas.

In terms of notation, I indicate possible finger substitutions, places to play a note with both fingers for added finger weight and/or special color effect, and hand or finger redistributions, as in m. 11 of "Doctor Gradus ad Parnassum."

Even if a student is playing only one piece of the suite, I would suggest reading through the entire commentary in order to get to know the piece as a whole, and to grasp issues that may not be movement-specific.

NOTES ON PERFORMING THE INDIVIDUAL PIECES

These notes are detailed mini-lessons as I would teach them to my students. They are not meant to be exhaustive, and, of course, I feel that they are just a starting point. There is a lot of room for thoughtful, informed interpretation and for the individual needs of any teacher and student. Those considerations are the stuff out of which each person will create a distinct and valuable performance. But through these notes I hope to point to the level of detailed thinking, listening, and examination that we need when we study Debussy's music.

In terms of a good order in which to introduce the various movements of the *Children's Corner* to less experienced students, I would suggest that one begin with "The little Shepherd." It is the simplest movement, but requires focused attention to finger touch and color control. Once these skills are mastered, I would continue with "Jimbo's Lullaby," then on to "Doctor Gradus ad Parnassum," "Serenade for the Doll," "Golliwogg's cake walk," and finally "The snow is dancing," which is technically the trickiest of the lot.

Doctor Gradus ad Parnassum

Gradus ad Parnassum is an important collection of piano studies composed by Muzio Clementi and published by him in 1817. Many generations of pianists, down to our present day, have encountered these valuable exercises. It is also the title of a compositional treatise by Johann Joseph Fux from 1725—J.S. Bach, Mozart, Haydn, and Beethoven were very familiar with this latter work. The title means "Steps to Parnassus," which in classical Greek mythology was the home of the nine Muses who were responsible for inspiration in the arts. By diligently practicing these exercises (taking them step by step), a student might achieve divinity—or at the very least proficiency—in his chosen art. While the obvious reference in Debussy's piece is to the Clementi exercises which he imagines a future Chou-Chou daydreaming her way through as she practices, there may be a private joke here as well in reference to Fux's venerable reputation. Debussy was very fond of ignoring the established rules of composition in favor of the sounds called for by his own remarkable sensibility.

The piece is full of opportunities to daydream in sound and color. It should sound moderately animated, but the tempo is completely a matter of taste. One can play fast and smoothly, as Debussy himself does in his recordings, or more slowly and with greater deliberation, as other great pianists do, in order to capture the impression they have of a little girl struggling with her technical exercises. I myself prefer to be on the side of Debussy's tempo and try to render a beautiful image of a young girl struggling with attention, not with execution. I imagine a dutiful beginning with an abrupt stop on the *sforzando* E of m. 12 as she turns the page resignedly and begins "the tricky, notey part," the slight flagging of attention and resumption of determined concentration in mm. 21 and 22, and the longing for release in the tender cross-hand melodies of mm. 24–31. From this beginning I am sure we can carry on quite imaginatively, all the way through the joyfully impatient coda that begins at m. 57 in which Chou-Chou speeds up to quickly finish her work and run outside to play. But all this must be suggested with charm and restrained expression—and above all, beauty and tenderness. In the end, it is not about how Chou-Chou is daydreaming; it is about how Debussy feels about how she looks while she is daydreaming. This removed artistic perspective is very French.

Although a spoof on the practicing of technical exercises, this piece does have great technical value: wrist motion towards the fourth and fifth fingers of the right hand, offering opportunities to make sure the wrist is behind and supporting each finger. It can be used as a study in collecting the fingers of the hand to ensure that we do not keep them extended, but rather that we allow the thumb to travel with the hand and use the circling motion of the wrist to get back to the thumb. This frees the fingers to be individually articulate—semi-legato, so that you can feel the highest notes of each group of sixteenth notes as a melody, with the notes underneath filling out harmonies. The notes themselves don't have to be released so evenly, but must be played rhythmically evenly (*égal*). The thumb can feel a harmonic line, caressing the key with a different and longer touch than the other fingers in order to produce a subtle harmonic color. The others depress the key at a faster rate, and the fourth finger will come out a little louder because it depresses and releases the key fastest. This understanding allows us to shape the patterns without any real dynamic changes, and we should hear and respond to the harmonies as they resolve from beat to beat. This attention to finger color and articulation also allows us to achieve a non-pedaled sound that is "without dryness" (*sans sécheresse*) as Debussy has directed. Using too much pedal here may completely swamp the excellent work of our fingers—but perhaps not, as we will see later in the piece.

m. 1 The opening grace note should already be in tempo, played as a sixteenth-note pickup to the patterns which follow. The LH thumb should be articulated with a pointed but gentle attack before changing to the fifth finger in *m. 2*.

m. 3 There should be a real difference between the last note of each group of sixteenths and the staccato melody (beginning on beat two). Similarly when the melody is written as legato quarter notes (*mm. 5–6*), hold the quarter notes using true finger legato, thus creating a different sound and color from the previous staccato notes. I use gentle and shallow pedaling for the staccato notes of *mm. 3–4* and deepen the pedaling for the legato notes of *mm. 5–6*, although I lighten the pedal in *m. 6* to allow room for the expressive decrescendo.

m. 7 Despite the use of pedal from the third or fourth sixteenth note of beat one, try for finger legato in both hands; especially try to hold the whole note F as long as possible. Just "thinking" the crescendo/decrescendo of this measure will be enough expression. What is more important is that there is no crescendo or decrescendo in the following measure. (Same for *mm. 9–10*) *m. 11* It is useful here and elsewhere to reorganize the hands to take more notes in the RH. Here it facilitates a nice rolling motion in the RH for complete legato. (Same in *mm. 55–64*)

m. 12 Allow the E to decrescendo before adding pedal. Many older editions mark the tied E on the downbeat of *m. 13* with a staccato. I personally like it and can defend it from an imaginative and musical standpoint, but Debussy himself ties it over without a staccato repetition. We should follow Debussy.

m. 14 Decrescendo past *piano* to come back to *piano* in *m. 15*. In *m. 16* just touch the LH G on the downbeat differently, with not too much crescendo, to demonstrate a different quality of crescendo. In *m. 17* lean on the tenuto slightly to hold it longer and give it a different color (hold it all the way through the A-sharp in the RH). Pedal is not necessary here if we finger pedal the F-sharp major triad in the RH.

m. 21 Observe that the staccato notes should sound slightly longer as the *retenu* unfolds; slip in the grace note of *m. 22* before the beat so that we hear the last D of the RH in *m. 21* resolve to the C on the downbeat of *m. 22*. Since we have let the pedal "out of the bag" since the beginning of the piece, I feel that we might as well use it in *m. 22* as preparation for the colors to come. This kind of pedaling is breathing, taking gentle breaths on each beat and quarter note that don't necessarily clear the sound completely. In *m. 23*, the LH uses true finger legato.

m. 24 Careful attention needs to be paid to the shaping of the LH cross-over notes and to make sure that the staccato C-sharp on beat three is truly a staccato and gentle sixteenth note, not part of the melody. This holds true for the following measure, with the important change of pedal on beat three mandated by the half rest in the bass voice. In *m. 26* make sure that these LH cross-over notes sound as tenuto quarter notes, not eighth notes. The articulation changes again in *m. 27*. In *m. 28* we should take care to use lots of flesh on the key for the legato LH melody notes.

m. 31 This scalelike passage ought to be like rainwater trickling down a pane of glass. Practice without pedal so you skim the surface of the key, each note a perfect pearl of sound, and don't let us hear the hand alternations. I would also strive to hold the G in the LH as long as possible.

m. 33 I throw the RH from the fourth finger to the thumb in order to use the RH on the treble clef notes, retaking the F of the bass clef in *m. 34* with the RH. This acrobatic execution allows us to keep contact with the LH B-flat throughout these two measures so we can change the pedal and hear the rest in the middle voice. We also need to keep in mind that we return to the first tempo here, although we are "dreaming." What keeps this entire section flowing and coherent is the bass line which has its origins in the upper voice of *m. 30*, descends through the scale of *m. 31* to the bass of *m. 32*, and from thence through the B-flat (*m. 33*) to the A-flat (*m. 37*) to the G octave in *m. 45*.

m. 35 The LH falling fourths ought to be well shaped and pronounced in such a way that they foreshadow the opening to "Jimbo's Lullaby." This prepares us for the dream world ushered in by the new harmonic color of *mm. 37–44*. We ought to caress the A-flat on the downbeat of *m. 37* with great tenderness. In *m. 38*, voice the LH top note (even though the tenuto is on the bottom of the chord), and take care to finish the phrase on the third beat of *m. 39*, being sensitive to the resolution of the harmony. In *m. 44* resolve the LH A-flat to the top G of the LH octave in *m. 45*. Be careful about voicing the thumb in the LH octave. I use no pedal because the octave is functioning as our pedal (both aurally and harmonically).

m. 57 En animant peu à peu does mean that we are to get livelier, but this does not mean just to play faster. The articulation of the fingers must contribute to the liveliness. The phrase starts on beat two, so we must be careful to finish our previous gestures without a bump on the downbeat. (Same in *m. 61*) Continue to use the hand redistribution because it helps keep the bottom voice legato. We should be aware of the sensitive echo of the LH melody by the last sixteenth note in each group.

m. 65 Observe dynamics especially in the RH. In *m. 68* the portato/staccato quarter note in the LH on beat one should be different from the heavy accents that follow. In *m. 71* the LH has two-note slurs and should be released after each. But in *m. 72* the LH is not slurred; all four notes should head for the downbeat of *m. 73*. I use two hands in *m. 76* (not just one, as is tempting) for better sound.

Jimbo's Lullaby

Jumbo was a plush stuffed elephant of Chou-Chou's; Debussy misspelled his name in the title of this movement. We can forgive him, however, since the French pronunciation of Jimbo does approximate the sound of Jumbo in English, as Roy Howat points out in the notes of his critical edition of *Children's Corner.* I have chosen to retain the misspelling because I feel it adds to the charm of the work—and anyway, it is what Debussy wrote at the time. In any case, every parent will recognize that this movement is really a lullaby for Chou-Chou with the obliging help of her pudgy friend.

m. 1 The LH should be played very legato, swung in a feeling of two; be sure to overlap the sound a little bit. The clumsiness (*gauche*) comes from the ponderous sound of the bass of the piano; again, we don't have to paint a literal picture or do too much to suggest the little elephant's awkward movements.

m. 4–5 Be careful about rhythm—even Debussy had problems in his recording. (Although I don't for a moment believe he was anywhere near as concerned with textual fidelity on recordings as we are today.) In *m. 4* treat the RH as a two-note slur, even though portato. This can be gently done as if nuzzling or tickling the child with the stuffed elephant. In *m. 5*, I touch the pedal on beat three to color the RH.

m. 9 Use the full una corda and keep the damper pedal depressed until the end of *m. 14*, as marked. This is one of Debussy's rare pedal indications. Only the RH should "ping," but in combination with the una corda. It is a magical color change. We should be careful about the voicing of the diads in *m. 10* and following; the G is more important than the F. In *m. 11–12* the reference to the French lullaby "Do, do, l'enfant do" ought to be played as legato as possible with the RH thumb. In *m. 15* use a two-note slur wrist technique ("down–up") to accomplish the crescendo.

m. 19 Most performers feel a more moving tempo here. I also enjoy very long pedals, with perhaps half changes every downbeat (*mm. 22–28*). Observe the tenuto on the second beat, allowing us to feel the swaying of the elephants. In *mm. 21–24* the RH is molto legato and felt in two beats per measure. Be careful of the voicing in *m. 25*, keeping the thumb (taking both notes of the diad) very soft.

mm. 32–33 Lean on the tenuto on the A-flat (fourth beat), but feel how the weight is transferred from the fifth finger to the thumb for an expressive legato. The RH chords need to be carefully voiced, with an expressive fifth finger marking the different

articulations. It is effective to treat the RH of *m. 34*, beats three and four, as a pedaled two-note slur, with a slightly snapped wrist on beat four to accomplish the *marqué* effect. This is also useful in the RH of *mm. 41–42*. Also snap the wrist for the *marqué* downbeat of *m. 45*, taking care to already be on the key with the fingers.

m. 39 More moving in a slightly lumbering fashion, as if clumsily making the stuffed elephant waddle or walk.

mm. 49–52 If we keep at least one voice legato from chord to chord (it doesn't have to be the same voice always, but this would be ideal), we can produce the illusion of finger legato without too much pedal.

m. 53 This *mezzo forte* is the loudest dynamic of the piece, and should sound like a real arrival. Imagine *m. 57* as slightly pompous and grand, listening to the ascending and descending inner and outer voices in the RH. In *mm. 59–60*, observe the RH crescendo/decrescendo on repeated B-flats, and the lack of them in the subsequent two measures. In *mm. 62–63*, make sure to hear the bass line D-flat–C-flat–B-flat; this will help grade the decrescendo and the *retenu.*

m. 64 Be sure to crescendo from the F to the D in the bottom voice of the RH. This is difficult to suggest but necessary to retain the integrity of the combination of the two melodies. In *m. 66* the thumb on beats three and four ought to be as legato as possible, without poking the sound and while keeping the upper voice absolutely legato.

m. 76 We should not slow down in the *morendo*, but rather should feel a suspension of the pulse (perhaps *mm. 78–80* should be felt as one big measure?), as if we are holding our breath while checking to make sure Chou-Chou is asleep before closing the door. The very last note is a long staccato and soft. We can start from the surface of the key for greater control of this hushed ending.

Serenade for the Doll

Obviously plucked and strummed, this most charming of movements contains many references to guitar playing. I always imagine Debussy, who was a significantly sized man, playing to a small doll on a small guitar for the pleasure of Chou-Chou who might have presented her doll to her father with the demand: "She wants a song." I favor a slower tempo than some of the older recordings for a more tender performance.

m. 1 and following Although played with alternate hands and staccato articulation throughout, it is useful to shape the two-note slurs, as you would with one hand, with a down–up motion in the wrists. The articulation is well played if thought of as lightly plucked, like a guitar. This articulation should be preserved, even when colored with pedal.

m. 3 There is a difference between not holding the grace notes here and holding them to form a chord, as Debussy asks in *mm. 6–7*. Here, and elsewhere, I would use the wrist to throw to the principal notes and to shape the phrase.

m. 8 and m. 14 Really *forte*! The continual use of the una corda produces an excellent effect and the *forte* serves to give some drama to this doll's story.

m. 26 The thumb articulation can be plucked or "twisted" out for the echo on beat two, but we must be sure to shape these echo notes. (Also in *mm. 27–29*)

m. 30 Despite the continued una corda, we can feel a sudden infusion of tenderness in the sound as the texture becomes richer.

mm. 35–43 Very careful attention to voicing will vastly increase the joy and beauty of these measures: especially the G-sharp–F-double sharp–B–A-sharp inner line of the RH; and the alternating C-sharp–D-sharp in the soprano, which is playfully treated in diminution in the LH top voice in *mm. 39–41*. It is also important to listen to the changes in the top voice in *mm. 39–41* and the bottom voice of the RH in *mm. 41–42*.

m. 53 The animation can come just as much from feeling the rests a little more strongly as from getting faster; but be sure to return to the original tempo at *m. 61*. If the *animant* is too fast, the return will sound abrupt, but it can be done with stylish elegance. *mm. 63–64* Listen for a good shape in the bass line.

m.66 There is an effective tradition to play this first roll *forte* instead of *piano*. *m. 69* Be sure to hold the top voices of the RH while strumming out the third beat, which should still be *pianissimo*. I use a bit of rhythmic pedal on all the *sforzandos* in *m. 72* and following. In *mm. 80–84*, it is a pleasure if we hear the repeated G-sharps change color as they move toward a tender resolution to the F-sharp on the downbeat of *m. 84*.

mm. 92–94 Note the differences in the quality of the dynamic markings—*piano* to *più piano* to *piano expressif*—three different kinds of *piano* dynamics! The *expressif* in *m. 94* refers to the LH melody; the RH continues in even time as a kind of metronome. We should observe carefully the subito *pianissimo* in *m. 97* and the different markings in *mm. 102–105*.

mm. 106–115 I find it useful to continue the two-note slur shape and technical idea (but not too pronounced) in the LH. *mm. 119–121* It is useful to shape the phrase according to the bass line D-sharp–G-sharp–E. I like to feel a decrescendo on the ascending arpeggio with the final E of the piece gently plucked *pppp* as an afterthought, from the surface of the key. The pedal indication in *m. 121* is Debussy's.

The snow is dancing

This evocation is a gentle toccata, portraying all the swirling and blowing types of snow: wet and dry, blinding and gentle, and gray and shining with reflected light. In regard to the use of pedal, several writers have recommended little or no pedal, and the piece sounds well this way. However, Debussy himself uses copious amounts of pedal in his recordings. I consider both practices successful; although if I begin without pedal, I find the necessary use of it in m. 14 (and similar places) to be jarring both aurally and logically since it interrupts the aural texture of the piece. Alfred Cortot's recording succeeds best in mixing the use of dry and pedaled sound to produce mini-squalls of blown snow, but he is in this respect, as in most others, incomparable and inimitable. Even if one chooses to use pedal (as I do), I would strongly recommend practice without pedal (as with all other pieces of any composer) in order to examine carefully the sound and articulations made by our fingers before possibly obscuring these by the use of pedal. This piece should show off the virtuosity and variety of our articulations and finger color, as if it were a "toccata," a piece about "touch."

m.1 and following It is important to hear the exact release of the eighth notes—precise eighth notes—especially if pedal is used. They should be as precise as tiny ice crystals, but as gentle as flakes of snow. The eighth notes should be shaped and played as one gesture.

m. 3 and following It is useful to point the thumb for a swift but soft attack on the whole notes; be sure to shape the phrase of whole notes. The final C-sharp in *m. 6* ought to have more tension because it is most dissonant. In *m. 7* note that the emphasized whole note changes voice to the bass of the LH and should be less accented than in previous measures.

mm. 11–12 This is a good example of layering, although we don't want to overemphasize it. Listen for the shape of the A–G–B-flat in the LH thumb. In *m.14* the jump to *mezzo piano* from the preceding dynamic is huge! A fast stroke (like plucking) for articulating the LH chords is useful. I find this section to be very joyful, like bells; the sky lightens a little bit. We should be sure to follow and shape the bass line down to the C-flat of *m. 16*, and similarly in the following measures.

mm. 20 and 21 I treat the LH patterns/leaps on beats three and four as two-note slurs, with a "down" on the chord and "up" on the thumb, wrist technique; the release of one staccato note propels you to the next.

m. 22 I treat this like a subito *piano*. The decrescendo of the previous measure just takes us to *mezzo piano*, not to *piano*. In any case the LH tenutos should be much lighter and shorter than those in the RH, as a kind of ghost or shaded color. Perhaps the sadness (*triste*) comes from wishing to be able to play outside, but not being able to. In *m. 23* I feel it is important to release the final note like the end of a phrase, even though it has a tenuto.

m. 30 We must be careful to accent just the thumb in the LH on the downbeat, not the bottom D as well. *m. 32* LH is staccato; make use of a throwing motion of the hand to avoid overstretching and tension in the hand. We must not crescendo too early, but should resist a crescendo down to the low C.

m. 34 and following I use a two-note slur technique ("down-up" wrist motion) to drop on the D–E-flat–F–G staccatos in the LH and release on the repeated C's (thus getting the C's for free, as it were). When this is comfortable, all eight notes of each beamed grouping can be practiced in one "down–up" gesture. The repeated C's also work well if played with the fourth finger. We can use this technique also in the LH of *m. 37*, where we should drop our thumb on the tenuto and get the second note of each group for free as well. For the RH triplets against the group of four notes in the LH, practice feeling the big beats as the rhythmic and technical impetus.

m. 40 A sudden release of the pedal on the downbeat will help define the rhythm of the lower staff. I find it useful to take the bottom staff with the RH and keep the LH playing the B-flat–C ostinato continuously until *m. 43*. This helps in keeping the hands together, but of course the LH and RH will continue to alternate as marked on the third and fourth beats of *m. 41* and *m. 43*. Note the rest in the LH on the fourth beat of *m. 43*!

mm. 47–49 Two-note slur wrist technique (down–up) will be useful for accomplishing this passage: down on beat two in both hands, up on beat three in both hands, etc. In *mm. 53–56*, try not to accent the downbeats, but instead try for an unbroken line.

mm. 64–65 The fingers of the RH must be held pretty flat underneath the LH, which should try to hold the half note as long a possible, especially in *m. 65*. It is useful to try to keep the LH wrist held high.

m. 69 I use the LH thumb as a pivot on the last sixteenth note of beat one in order to throw the hand upwards to the fourth finger on the G-flat of beat two.

mm. 72–73 It is advisable to hear the A in the LH resolve to the D every other note; use a delicate articulation here—a flick of the staccato notes with the finger tips in the LH. The final roll should be relatively fast, in keeping with the *sans ralentir*. It is good to gradually release the pedal while holding the notes with the fingers.

The little Shepherd

These images—a painting of the outdoors, surely; the flute or pipe of a shepherd in the hills or mountains; his dancing (or the prancing of sheep); the colors of the sunset; and the echoes from the rocks in the hills—come to life for Chou-Chou as she plays with her toy shepherd, or perhaps reads about him.

As a general rule, we should first practice the opening soliloquy in strict time to learn the rhythm. But we must take care to understand the musical gestures and learn to play in relation to musical shapes, not strict metronomic rhythm. We should also feel how the longer notes hang in the air, like the very first G-sharp, or are wafted back up after a descent (e.g., in the last B to B gesture of *m. 1*, wherein we can feel a real transfer of hand weight).

mm. 3 and 4 It is important not to play the grace notes too fast, but to make them melodic so we can hear the different shadings of color and the crescendos/decrescendo Debussy asks for. Note that *mezzo forte* is a very loud dynamic in this piece.

mm. 1–4 To use no pedal is an option; however, with a sensitive ear and a good piano, tiny pedals in the first few measures are the pianist's answer to vibrato on the flute. We are also able to smear the pedal the tiniest bit at certain points in this extended phrase, as if we are softening the outlines of a chalk drawing.

m. 7 It will be sufficient if we just "think" the poco crescendo and decrescendo. In *mm. 10–11* (and similar places), we can just caress the LH and RH with a feather touch, playing in such a way that they add to the sunset purple sonority as resonance, complementing the chord on the downbeat, not as sounds which compete with it. The measures immediately following the *cédez* (also *mm. 17–18* and *30–31*) should perhaps feel as if they have no tempo (they are just "color" measures), but we should practice them in time to understand their relationship to the main tempo of the piece. I like to hear them played languorously in a slower tempo set up by the *cédez*.

m. 14 On beats one and two in the LH, I suggest that we choose LH fingering depending on what gives us the best voicing for our hand and piano. In *mm. 14–15*, I try to shape the top voice and bass of the LH chords like an hourglass, feeling the different harmonies of each chord.

mm. 24–26 It might be advisable to come back to some semblance of the original tempo. However, it is more important to feel the pulse in two beats per measure, with the game being that we need an exact and strict echo on the second half of each of *mm. 24 and 25*.

Golliwogg's cake walk

Chou-Chou possibly owned a little black doll (in vogue at the time) with exaggerated red lips, flexibly jointed limbs akimbo, and a wildly tossed head of hair; or she might have owned one of the very popular books by Florence Upton which detailed the adventures of the little black Golliwoggs, as they were named. In either case, Debussy capitalizes on the crisp and energetic movements of this originally American dance developed by African slaves in the nineteenth century. It was meant as a high-spirited and grossly exaggerated parody of the ballroom

dancing popular among the wealthy land owners. The dancers would combine high kicking steps with short hopping movements and wear outsized bow ties, hats, and other formal wear. Debussy mixed these characteristics with the stylized and sometimes slapstick gags of the American vaudeville blackface minstrel shows which were wildly popular in Paris. It offered a platform for his own sarcastic humor, aimed at the overwhelming musical influence wielded by German composers of the day, especially the late Richard Wagner. The central section of this cake walk mercilessly parodies the opening of *Tristan und Isolde*, one of Wagner's most famous operas, which opens with this famous harmonic progression:

Tristan und Isolde

Debussy turns this into a ridiculous series of exaggerated jokes. I am indebted to Jean-Louis Haguenauer for the brilliant notion that mm. 47–60 might be heard as old man Wagner himself, hobbling along on a crutch. We can hear Debussy almost say, with the creeping bass of m. 61, "Hear comes that old and tiresome Tristan again." And, after completely ruining Wagner's innovative harmonies with grand and exaggerated emotion (so appropriate in a cake walk), his shoulders shake with barely suppressed laughter. Debussy repeats his point often enough to thoroughly ridicule both Wagner and his influence, before returning to the irrepressible fun of the cake walk proper in m. 92.

In performing this piece, Debussy's recording reveals very snapped rhythms and an energetic tempo. The pulse should be very steady and "just," but the pronunciation of the rhythms ought to be quite stylish and clear. Attention should be paid to the minute differences in articulation (i.e., the difference between the staccato second note of m. 1 and the non-staccato second note of m. 2). However, I don't want to encourage an overly exaggerated and "nice" execution, which would ruin the energy of the piece.

mm. 2–3 We should take care to play with sharp rhythmic accents on the C-flat. However, note the different accent on the C-flat of *m. 4*, which should be leaned into in preparation for a very sharp and short attack on the last *sforzando* chord of the measure.

m. 6 We must be careful not to play each beat with the same accent; beat two in a 2/4 measure is always less than the downbeat, even if only slightly so. I push inward on the repeated RH notes to accomplish the crescendo.

m. 25 Two-note slur wrist technique is useful (down–up), and leading with the thumbs in both hands will help in navigating the leap.

m. 38 Some pedal may be nice here, but it wouldn't have to be used as long as we make sure to hold the tied half notes for their full value into the next measure.

m. 47 This section must truly be played at a slower tempo than the opening allegro. We must be sure to articulate the grace notes clearly, especially so we hear the A-natural in the RH of *m. 48*. Anchor the thumb in the LH so that the LH staccato can be light and bouncy. *m. 52* Hold the LH D-flat for its full value and then immediately release it on the downbeat of *m. 53*.

mm. 61–62 The crescendo goes all the way to the downbeat of *m. 63*, enhancing the surprise of the subito *piano*. In *m. 63* and similar measures, be sure to use pedal to sustain the chords at least to the next measure.

mm. 71–72 A useful aid in remembering this passage is to follow with our ear the scale played by our RH thumb, taking care not to drown out the melody. The voice leading of this entire section, *mm. 61–92*, deserves close attention for its interconnected inner lines. In *m. 88*, observe the F resolution in the RH thumb, which is part of the scalelike line beginning in the RH thumb of *m. 81* and extending all the way in our ear to the G played by the LH in *m. 92*. In *mm. 71–72* and similar measures (including *mm. 85–86*), pedaling is determined by the need to sustain the half notes.

m. 111 I try for a change of color by playing the bottom two notes in the RH softer than their corresponding notes in the previous measure, while at the same time making the top voice crescendo, thus honoring the spirit of Debussy's markings.

m. 113 Be sure to observe the resolution in the RH thumb.

Notes

1. Long, *At the Piano with Debussy*, p. 58.
2. Ibid., pp. 59–60.

References

Dumesnil, Maurice. *How to Play and Teach Debussy*. New York: Schroeder and Gunther, Inc., 1932.

Long, Marguerite. *At the Piano with Debussy*, trans. Olive Senior-Ellis. London: J.M. Dent and Sons Ltd., 1972.

Raad, Virginia. *The Piano Sonority of Claude Debussy*. Lewiston/Queenston/Lampeter: The Edwin Mellen Press, 1994.

Audio Credits

Steinway Piano
David Lau, Recording Engineer
SunAh Lee, Producer

Acknowledgements

I am greatly indebted to both Karen Taylor and Jean-Louis Haguenauer for several important discussions about Debussy, in general, and the *Children's Corner*, in particular. Nelita True and Menahem Pressler taught me how to love and hear it, but it was my mom, who let me pilfer her old, beat-up Durand copy, who really started it all. So—thanks, mom.

Children's Corner

*À ma chère petite Chouchou avec les tendres excuses de son Père pour ce qui va suivre.**

I. Doctor Gradus ad Parnassum

Modérément animé [♩ = 144]

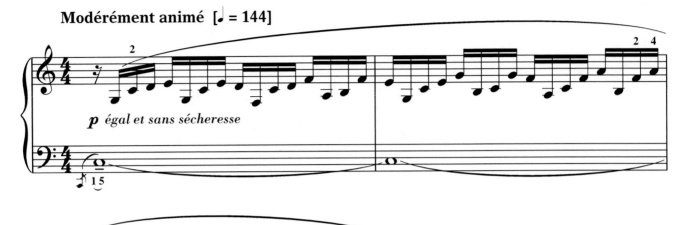

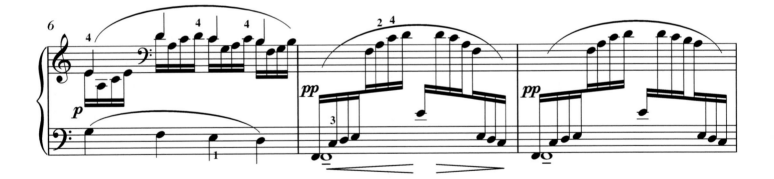

To my dear little Chouchou with the tender excuses of her father for that which follows.

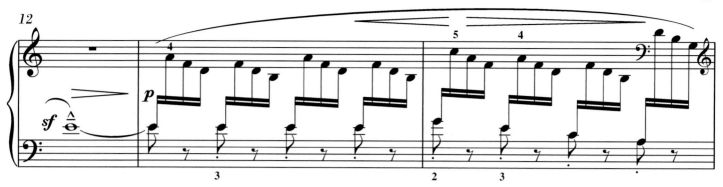

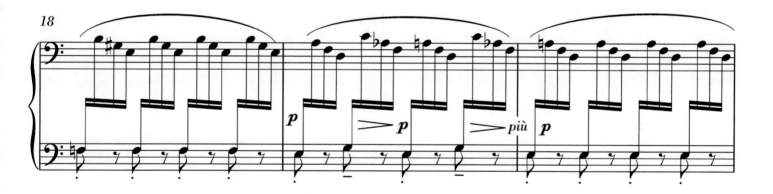

un peu retenu // *a tempo*

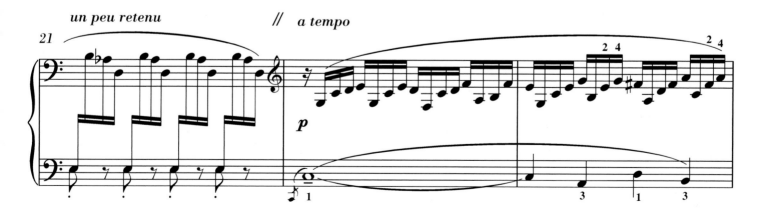

18

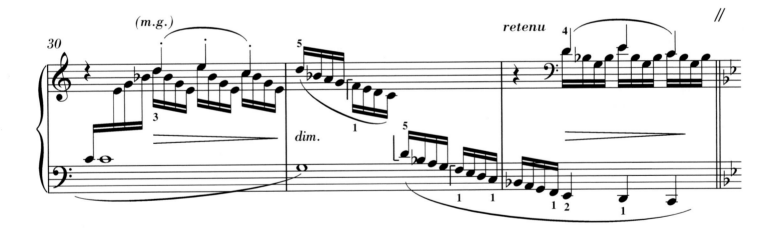

1° Tempo

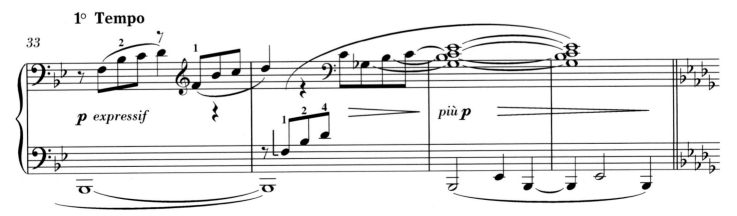

*play with both fingers.

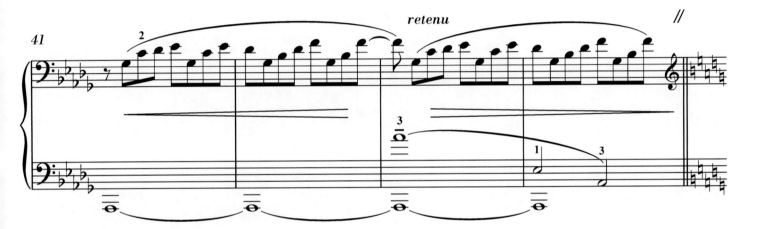

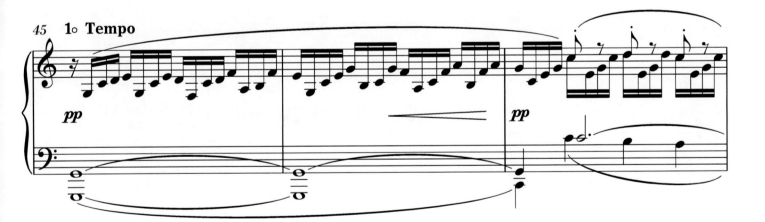

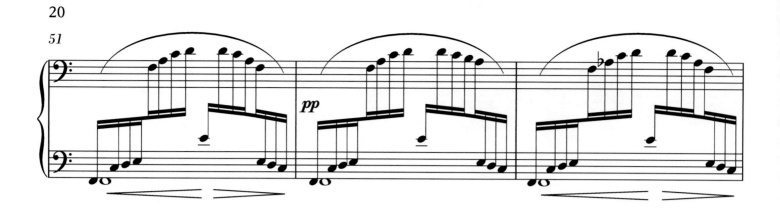

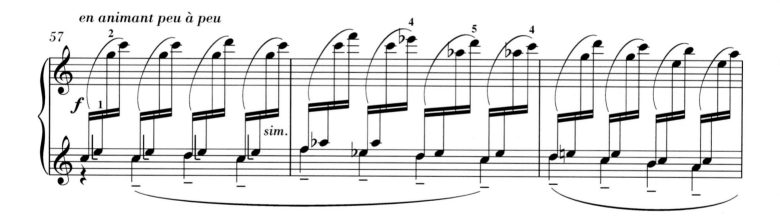

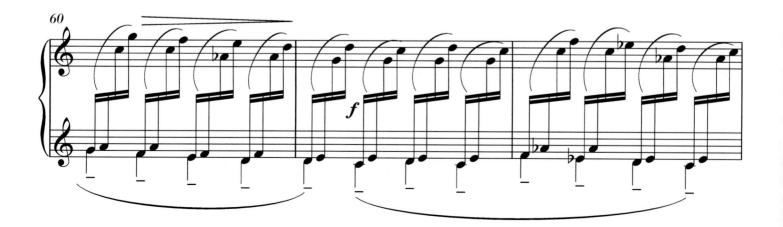

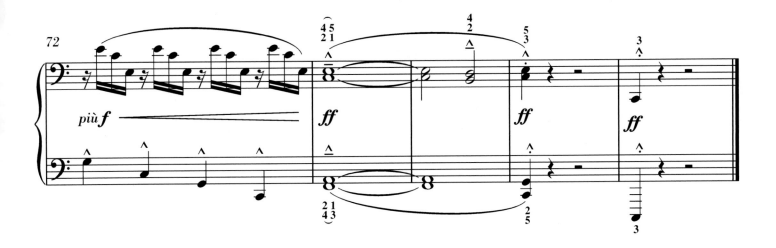

22

II. Jimbo's Lullaby

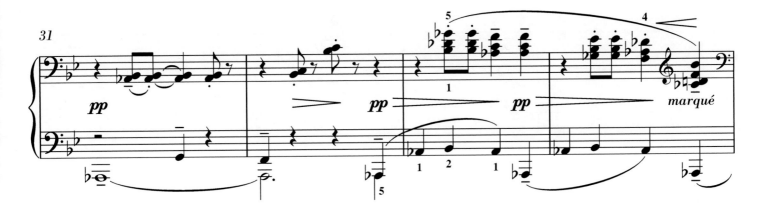

un peu plus mouvementé [♩ = 69]

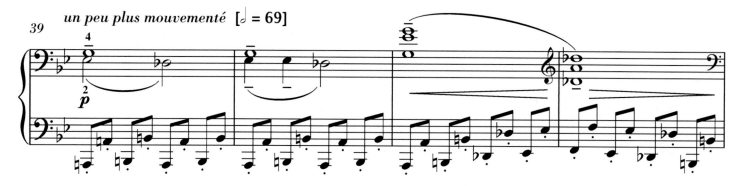

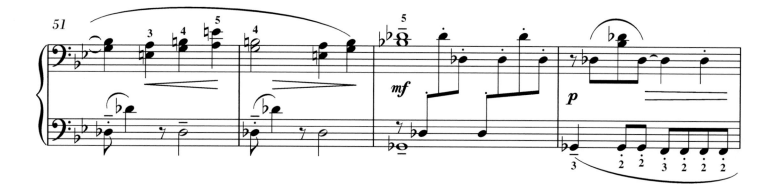

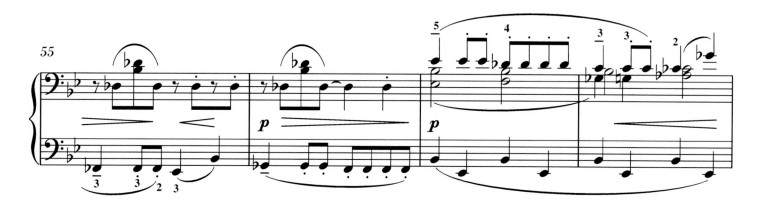

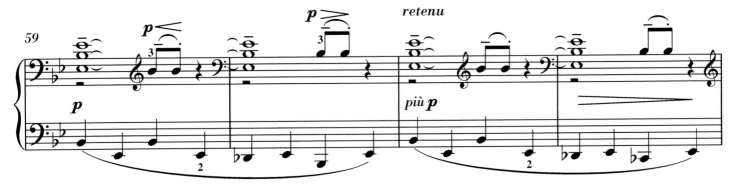

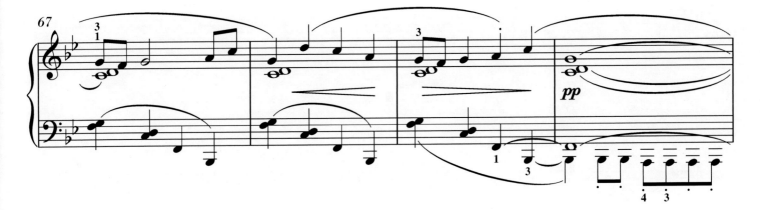

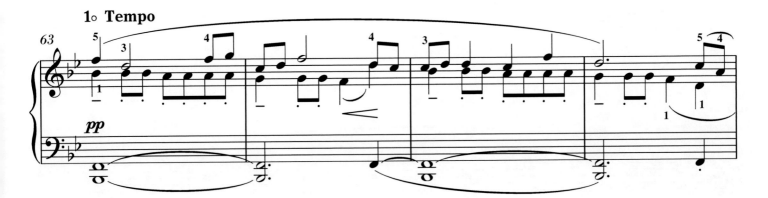

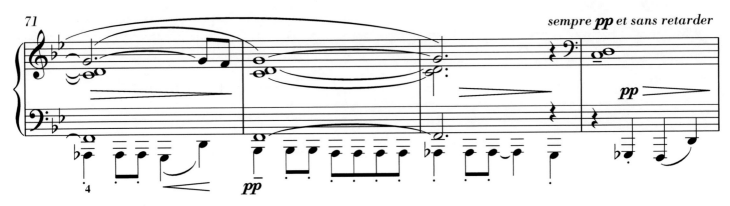

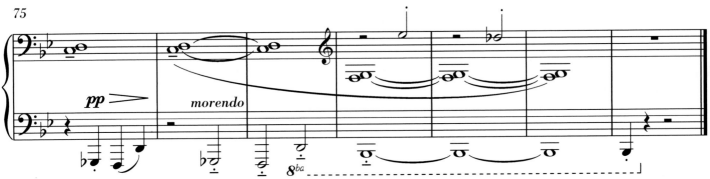

III. Serenade for the Doll

Allegretto ma non troppo [♩ = 152]

* Tres léger et gracieux

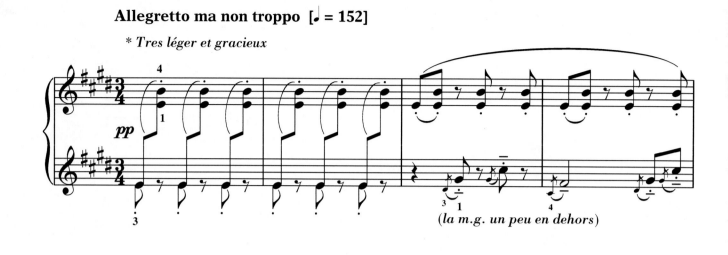

(la m.g. un peu en dehors)

(la m.d. un peu en dehors)

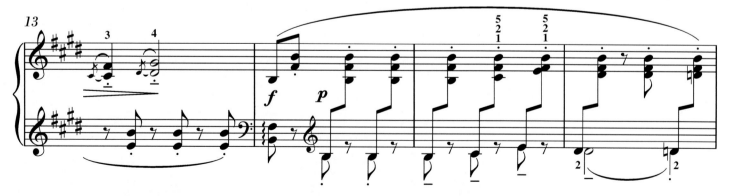

** Il faudra mettre la pédale sourde pendant toute la durée de ce morceau, même aux endroits marqués d'un **f**.*
*(It is necessary to use the una corda during the entire piece, even in the places marked **f**.)*

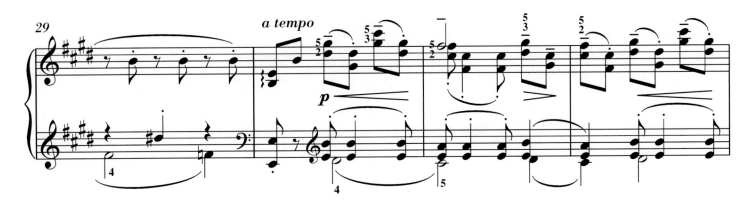

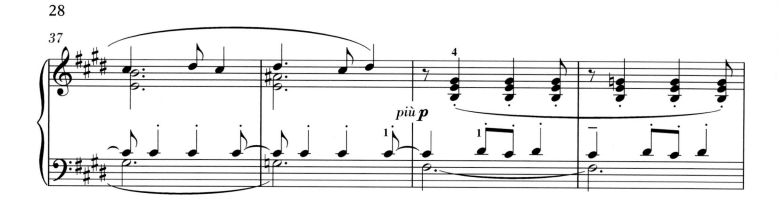

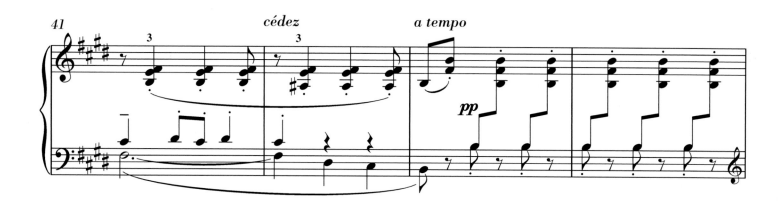

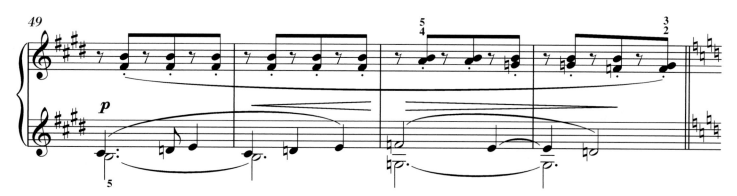

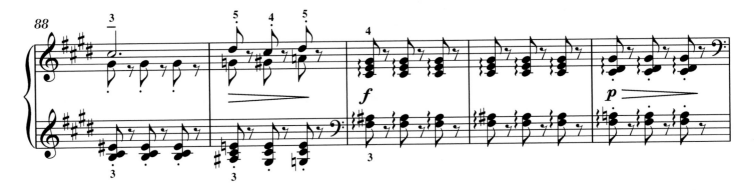

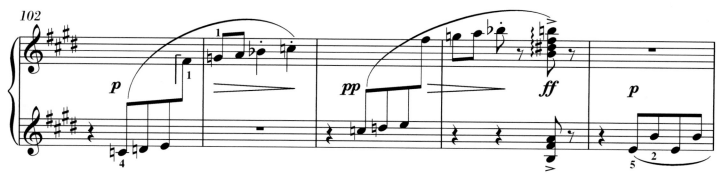

IV. The snow is dancing

Modérément animé [♩ = 132]

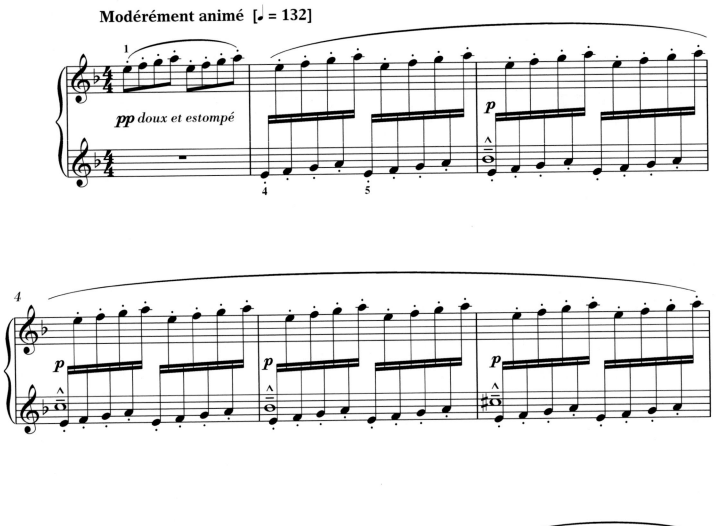

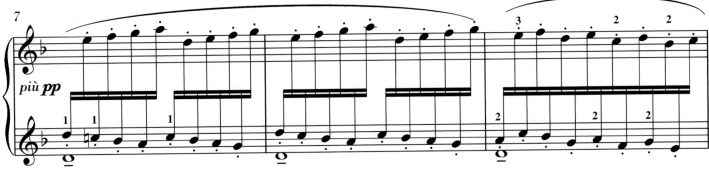

(LH above)

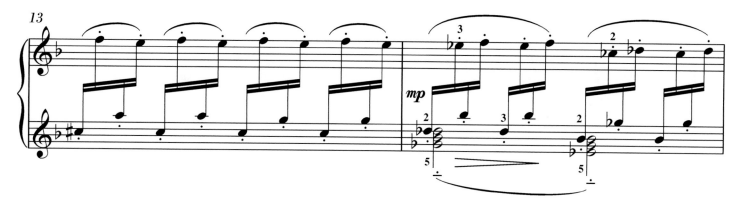

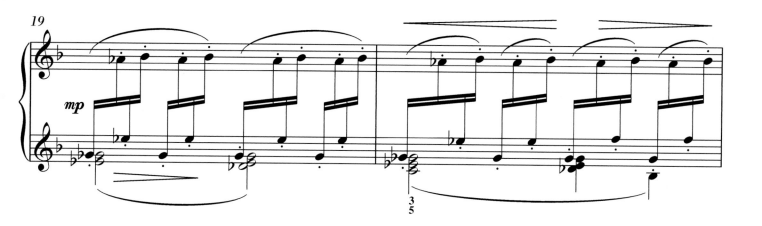

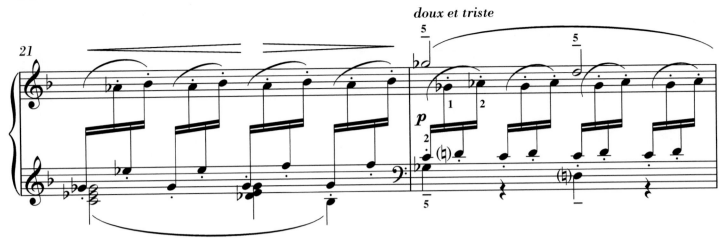

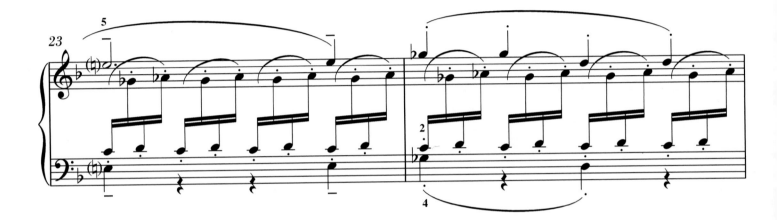

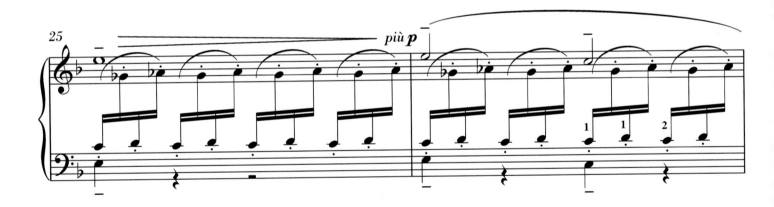

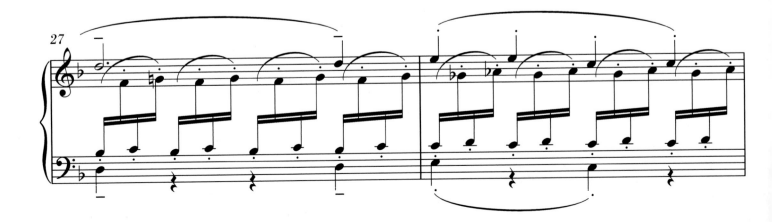

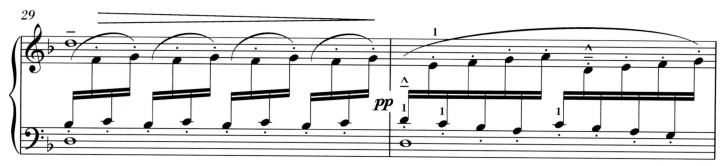

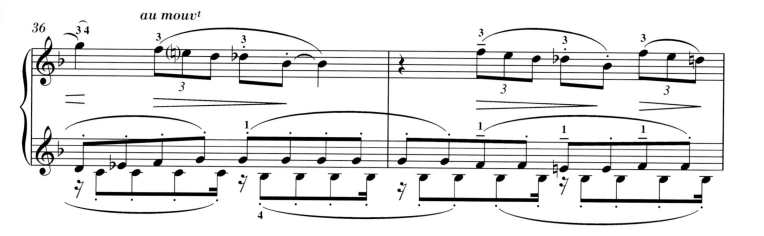

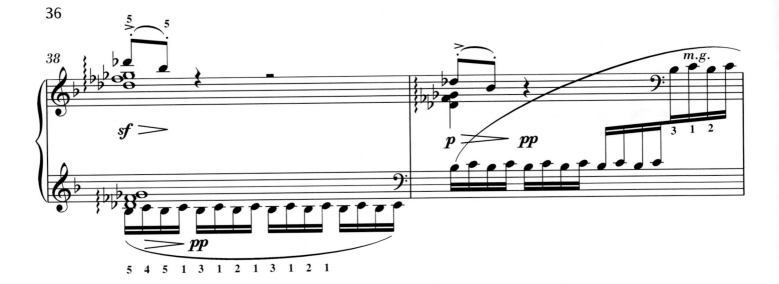

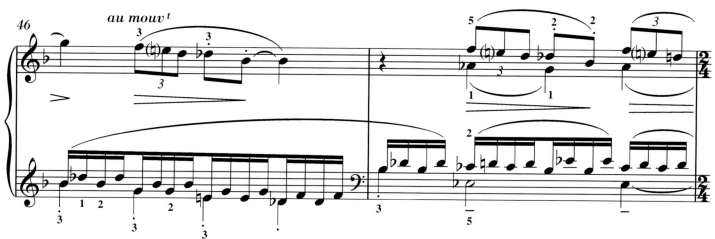

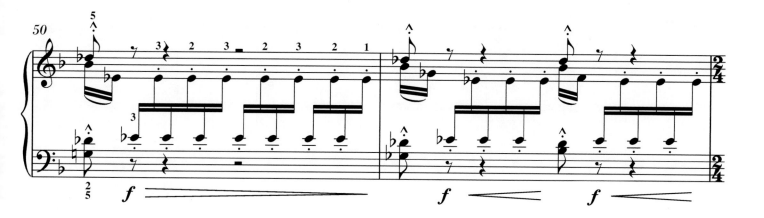

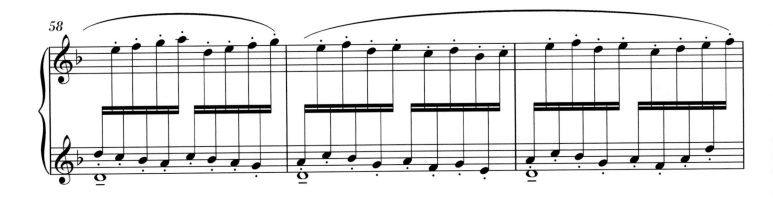

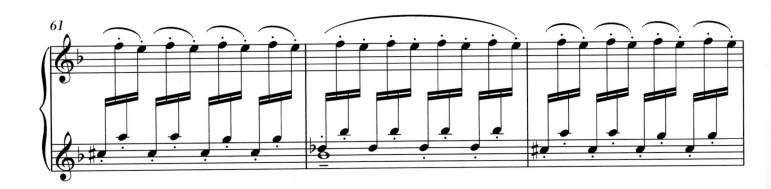

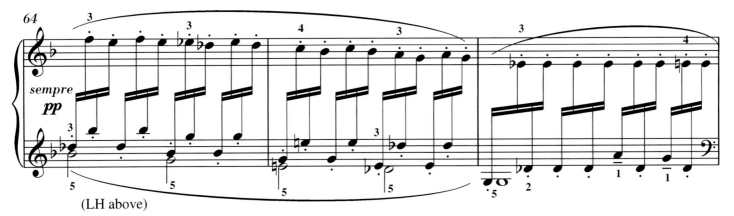

(LH above)

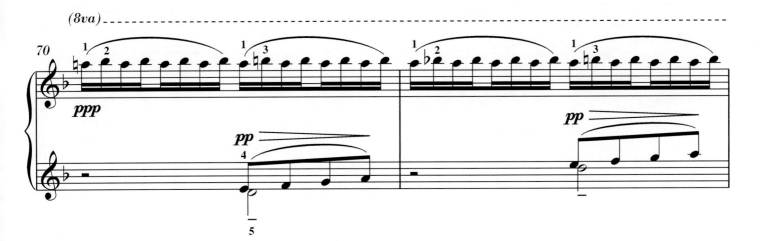

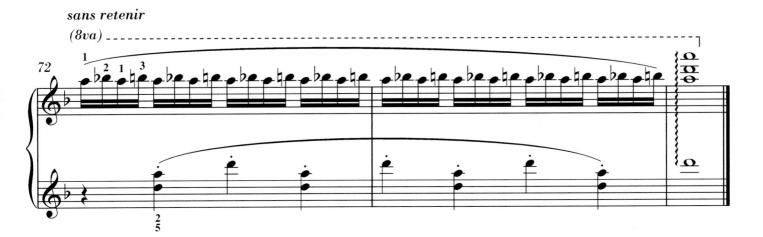

V. The little Shepherd

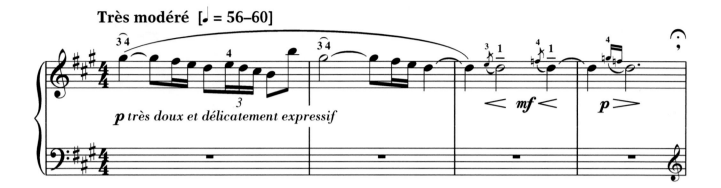

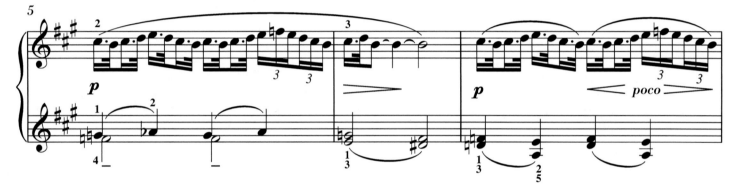

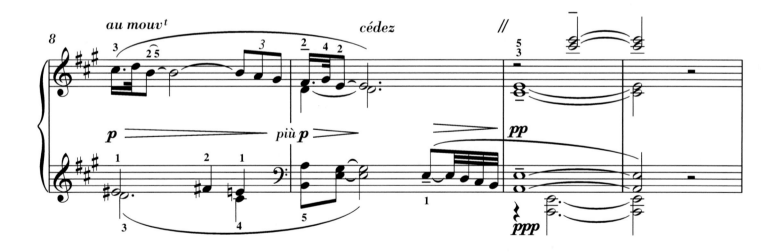

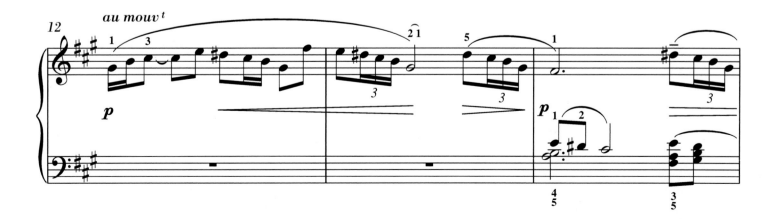

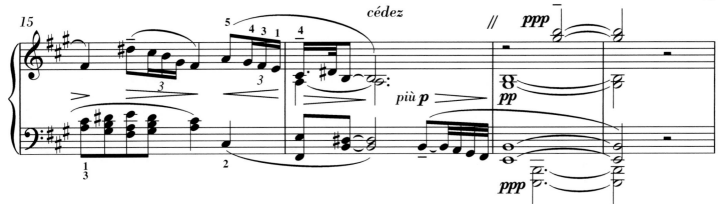

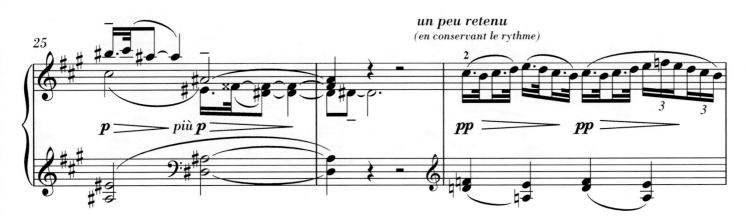

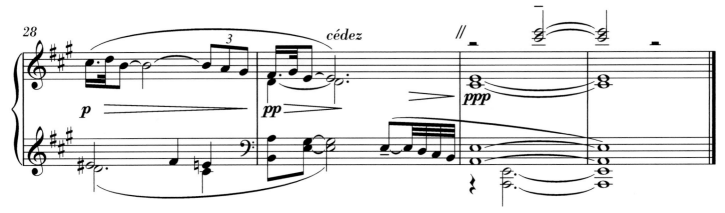

VI. Golliwogg's cake walk

Allegro giusto [♩ = 112]

très net et très sec

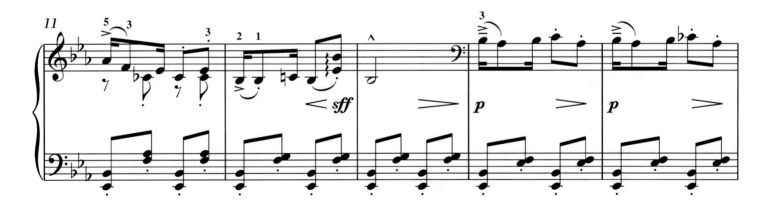

un peu moins vite

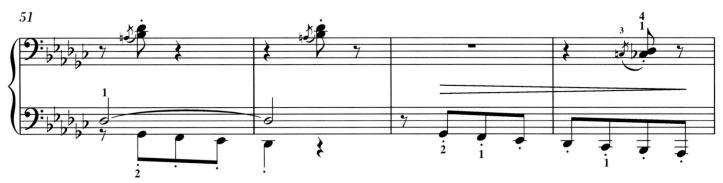

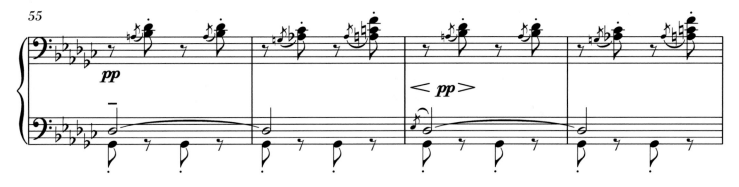

cédez
p avec une grande émotion

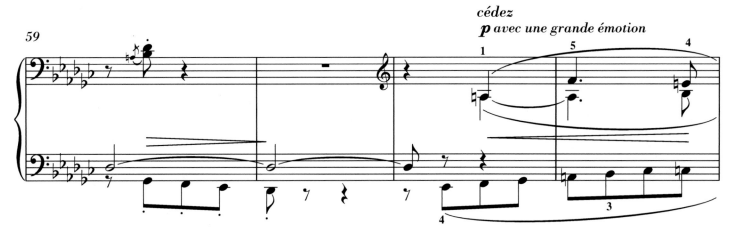

a tempo   *cédez*   *a tempo*

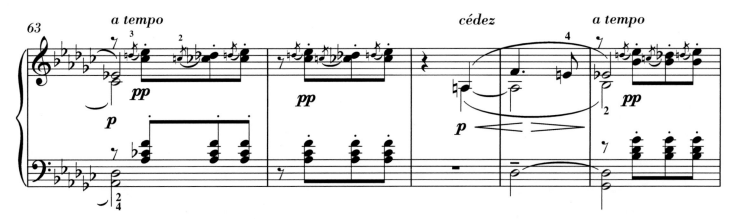

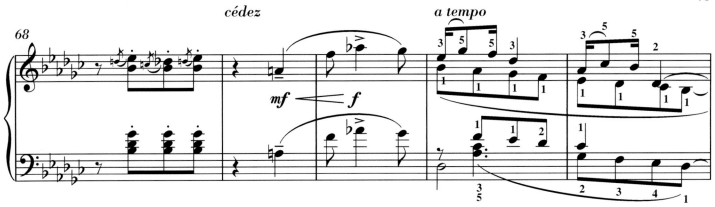
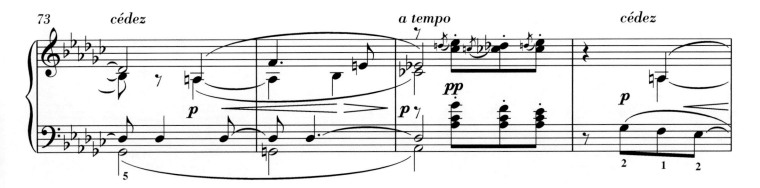
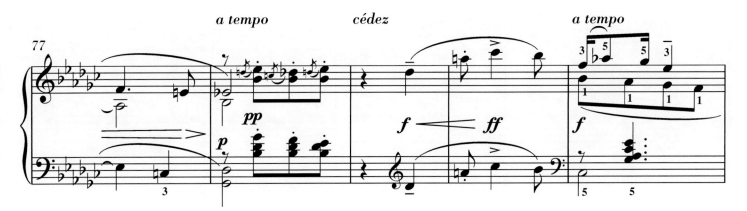

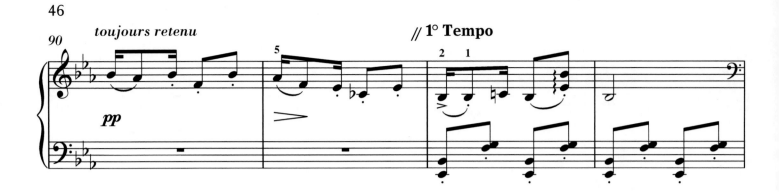

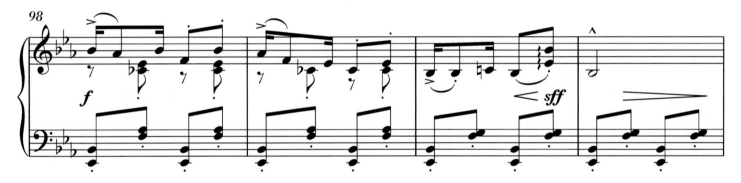

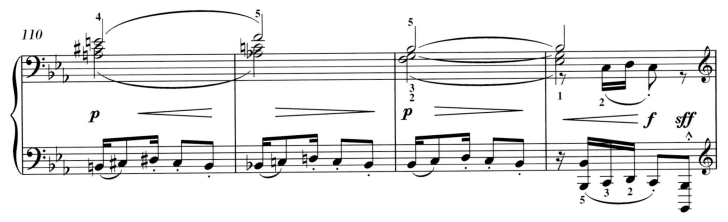

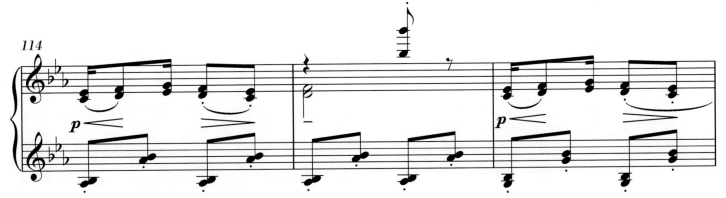

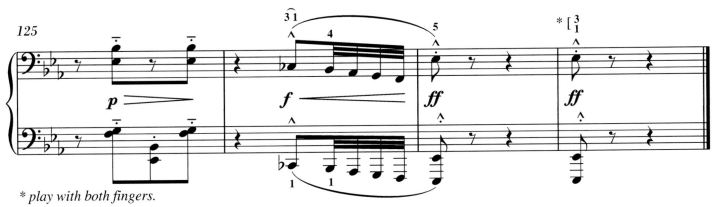

* *play with both fingers.*

APPENDIX

Doctor Gradus ad Parnassum
(with editor's suggested pedaling)

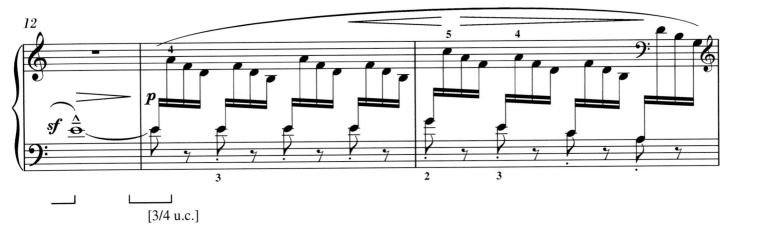

[3/4 u.c.]

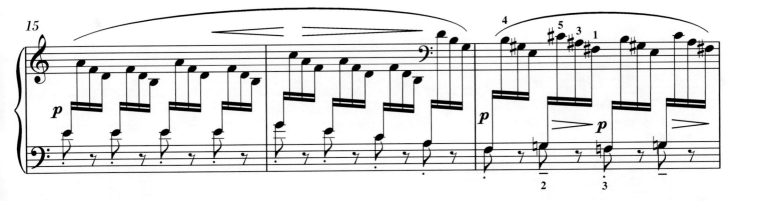

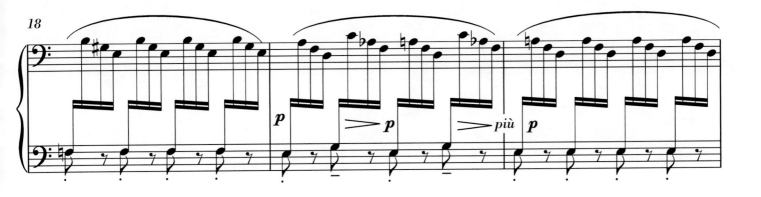

un peu retenu // *a tempo*

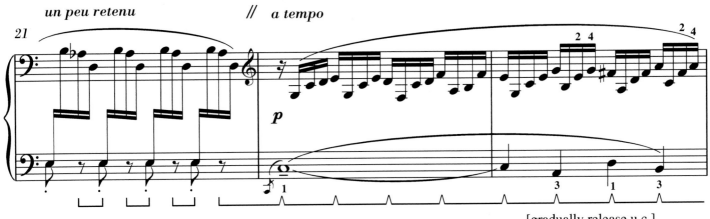

[gradually release u.c.]

[gradually 3/4 u.c.]

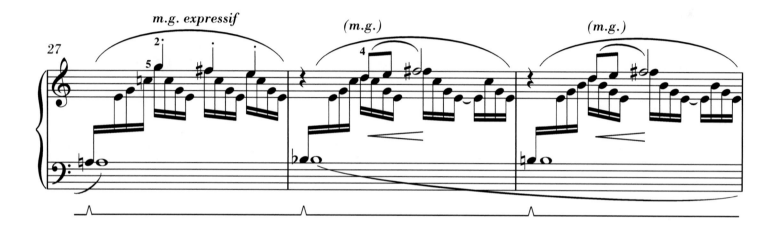

1° **Tempo**

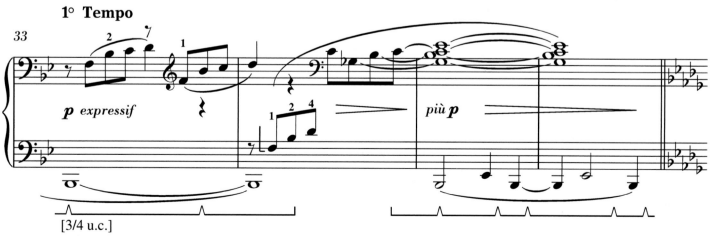

[3/4 u.c.]

*play with both fingers.

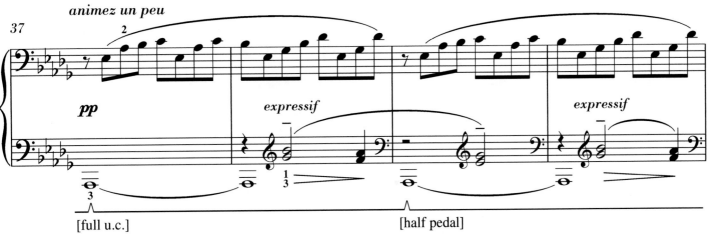

[full u.c.] [half pedal]

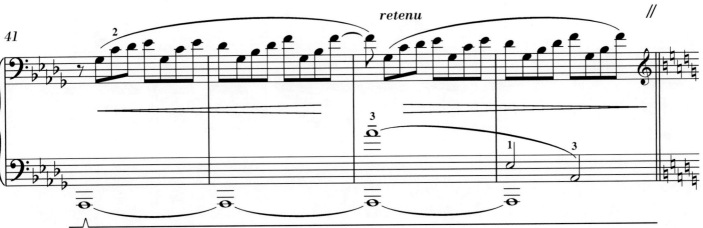

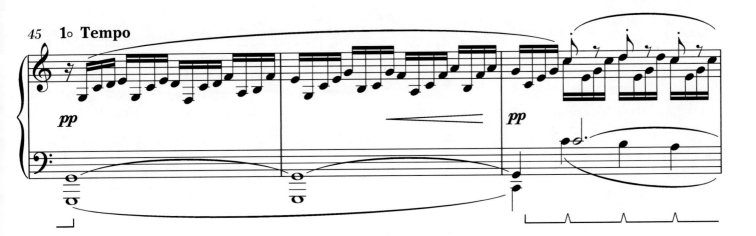

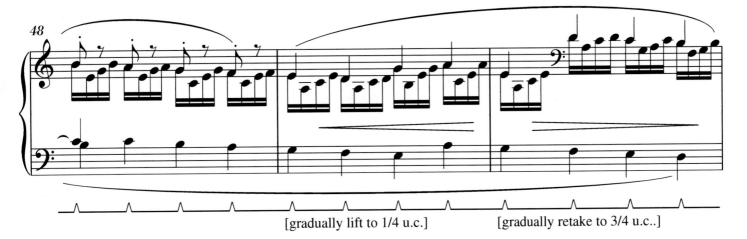

[gradually lift to 1/4 u.c.] [gradually retake to 3/4 u.c..]

52

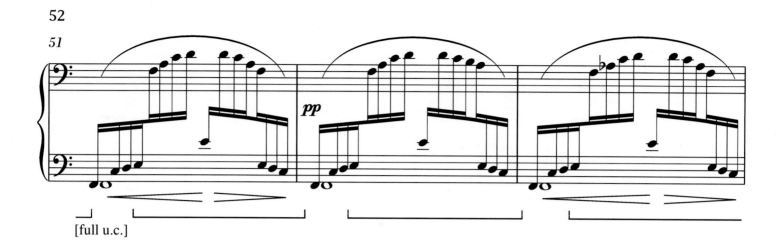

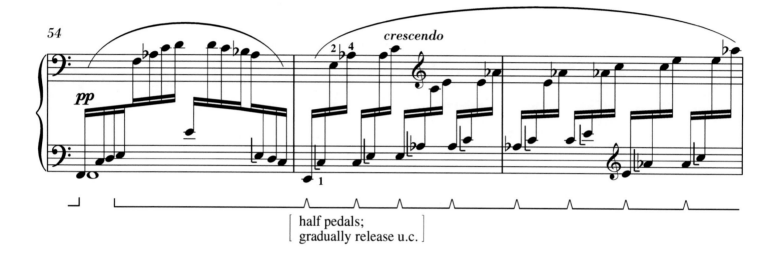

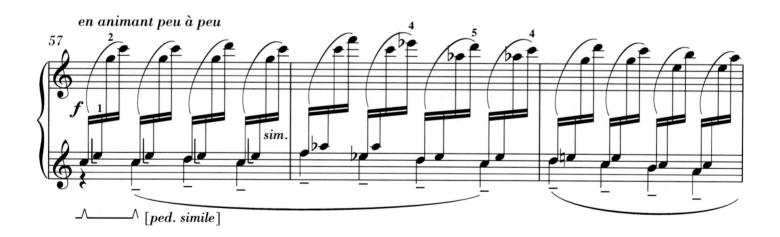

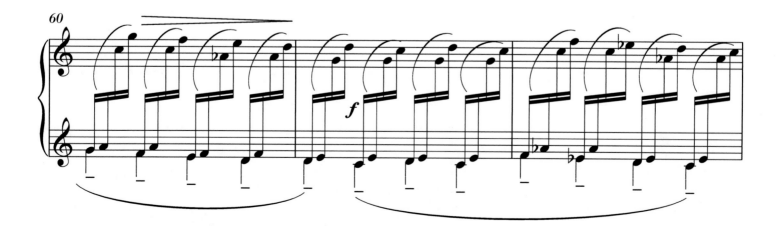

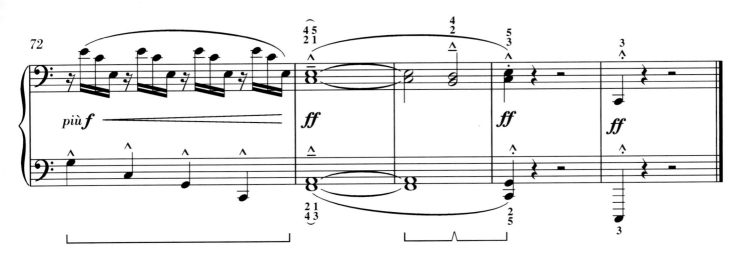

GLOSSARY OF FRENCH TERMS

FRENCH	ENGLISH
animez un peu	quicken a little
assez modéré	rather moderately
au mouvt (au mouvement)	return to the original tempo
avec une grande emotion	with exaggerated emotion
cédez	gradually slowing
cédez un peu	slowing down a little
doux et estompé	sweet and muted
doux et triste	sweet and sad
doux et un peu gauche	sweet and a little clumsy
égal et sans sécheresse	even and without dryness
en animant peu à peu	getting livelier little by little
en animant un peu	getting a little more lively
en conservant le rythme	but still play rhythmically
expressif	expressive
léger, mais marqué	light, but marked
les 2 Ped.	the two pedals, una corda and damper
m.d. (main droit)	right hand
m. g. (main gauche)	left hand

FRENCH	ENGLISH
la m.d. un peu en dehors	bring out the right hand a little
la m.g. un peu en dehors	bring out the left hand a little
marqué	marked
modérément animé	moderately animated
plus mouvementé	more animated
retenu	held back
sans retarder	without slowing down
sans retenir	without holding back
sempre pp et sans retarder	always very soft and without slowing down
toujours retenu	always holding back, getting slower
très animé	very quick
très doux et délicatement expressif	very sweet and delicately expressive
très léger et gracieux	very light and graceful
très modéré	very moderately
très net et très sec	very clear and very dry
un peu en dehors	a little brought out
un peu moins vite	a little less fast
un peu plus mouvementé	a little more animated
un peu retenu	a little held back
1^0 Tempo	return to the original tempo

ABOUT THE EDITOR

CHRISTOPHER HARDING

Christopher Harding is on the artist faculty of the University of Michigan, School of Music, Theatre, and Dance. He has performed internationally and across the United States, generating enthusiasm and impressing audiences and critics alike with his substantive interpretations and pianistic mastery. He has given frequent solo, concerto, and chamber music performances in venues as far flung as the Kennedy Center and Phillips Collection in Washington DC, Suntory Hall in Tokyo, the National Theater Concert Hall in Taipei, the Jack Singer Concert Hall in Calgary, and halls and festival appearances in Newfoundland and Israel. His concerto performances have included concerts with the National Symphony and the Saint Louis Symphony Orchestras, the San Angelo and Santa Barbara Symphonies, and the Tokyo City Philharmonic, working with such conductors as Taijiro Iimori, Gisele Ben-Dor, Fabio Machetti, Randall Craig Fleisher, John DeMain, Ron Spiegelman, Daniel Alcott, and Darryl One, among others. His chamber music and duo collaborations have included internationally renowned artists such as Karl Leister, András Adorján, and members of the St. Lawrence and Ying String Quartets, in addition to frequent projects with his distinguished faculty colleagues at the University of Michigan. He has recorded two solo discs and one chamber music disc for the Brevard Classics label.

Professor Harding has presented master classes and lecture recitals in universities across the United States and Asia, as well as in Israel and Canada. Additionally, he has extensively toured China under the auspices of the U.S. State Department, and was in residence at the Sichuan Conservatory of Music as a Fulbright Senior Specialist at the invitation of the American Consulate in Chengdu, China.

Mr. Harding was born of American parents in Munich, Germany, and raised in Northern Virginia. He holds degrees and Performer's Certificates from the Eastman School of Music and the Indiana University School of Music. His collegiate studies were with Menahem Pressler and Nelita True. Prior to college, he worked for ten years with Milton Kidd at the American University Department of Performing Arts Preparatory Division, where he was trained in the traditions of Tobias Matthay. He has taken twenty-five first prizes in national and international competitions, and in 1999 was awarded the special Mozart Prize at the Cleveland International Piano Competition, given for the best performance of a composition by Mozart.